Wild Outdoors

Freshwater Fishing

by Carol K. Lindeen

Reading Consultant: Barbara J. Fox
Reading Specialist
North Carolina State University

Content Consultant: Greg Slone
Next Generation Hunting
Bowling Green, Kentucky

CAPSTONE PRESS
a capstone imprint

Blazers is published by Capstone Press,
151 Good Counsel Drive, P.O. Box 669, Mankato, Minnesota 56002.
www.capstonepub.com

 Books published by Capstone Press are manufactured with paper
containing at least 10 percent post-consumer waste.

Library of Congress Cataloging-in-Publication Data
Lindeen, Carol K., 1976-
  Freshwater fishing / by Carol K. Lindeen.
      p. cm. — (Blazers. Wild outdoors)
  Includes bibliographical references and index.
  Summary: "Describes the equipment, skills, and techniques needed for freshwater fishing"—
Provided by publisher.
  ISBN 978-1-4296-4810-3 (library binding)
  1. Fishing—Juvenile literature. I. Title. II. Series.

SH445.L56 2011
799.1'1—dc22   2010001015

Editorial Credits

Christine Peterson, editor; Veronica Correia, designer; Sarah Schuette, photo stylist;
    Marcy Morin, scheduler; Laura Manthe, production specialist

Photo Credits

Alamy: prettyfoto, 29, Steve May, 27, Tom Thulen, 10, 24; Capstone Press: Gary Sundermeyer, 12
(bottom), 15 (middle, top), 19; Capstone Studio: Karon Dubke, 13, 16, 26 (bottom, both); Getty
Images Inc.: Johner Images/Jeppe Wikstrom, 22, The Image Bank/Burton McNeely, 6, Visuals
Unlimited/Wally Eberhart, 5, 7; iStockphoto: Steve Cole, 9; Shutterstock: Dewitt, 14, Doctor
Kan, 25, Fedor Kondratenko, 15 (bottom), Jens Stolt, 12 (top), Mike Flippo, 26 (top), NWH, 9
(inset), 20, Peter Zacher, cover

Artistic Effects

Capstone Press/Karon Dubke (woods); Shutterstock: rvika (wood), rvrspb (fence), VikaSuh (sign)

Printed in the United States of America in Stevens Point, Wisconsin.
102010
005977R

Table of Contents

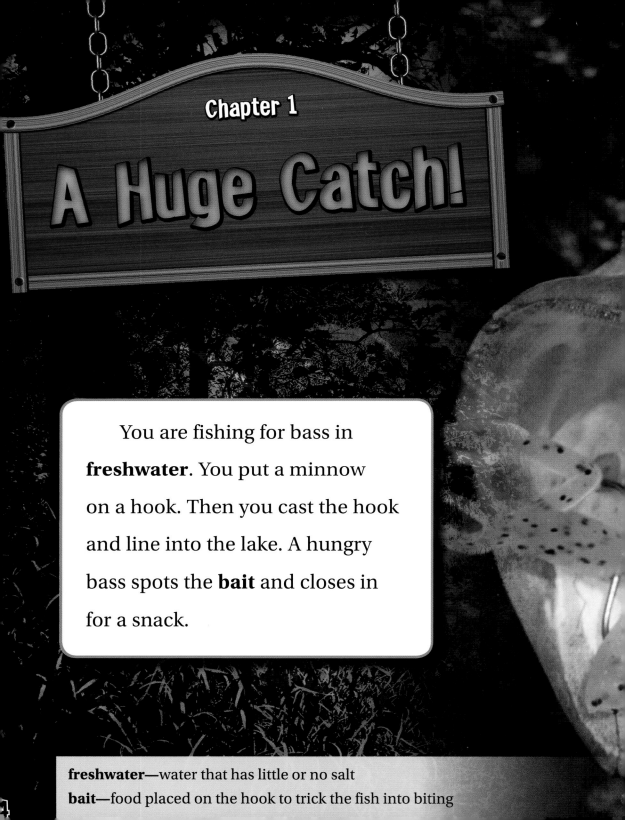

Chapter 1

A Huge Catch!

You are fishing for bass in **freshwater**. You put a minnow on a hook. Then you cast the hook and line into the lake. A hungry bass spots the **bait** and closes in for a snack.

freshwater—water that has little or no salt
bait—food placed on the hook to trick the fish into biting

Fish are often found near objects in the water like boat docks, rocks, and trees.

Quickly, you snap the rod. The rod's motion sets the hook in the fish's jaw. The bass struggles to escape. The rod bends with the fish's weight. Time to reel in the catch.

Wild Fact:

Freshwater fishers reel in big catches from lakes, ponds, rivers, and streams.

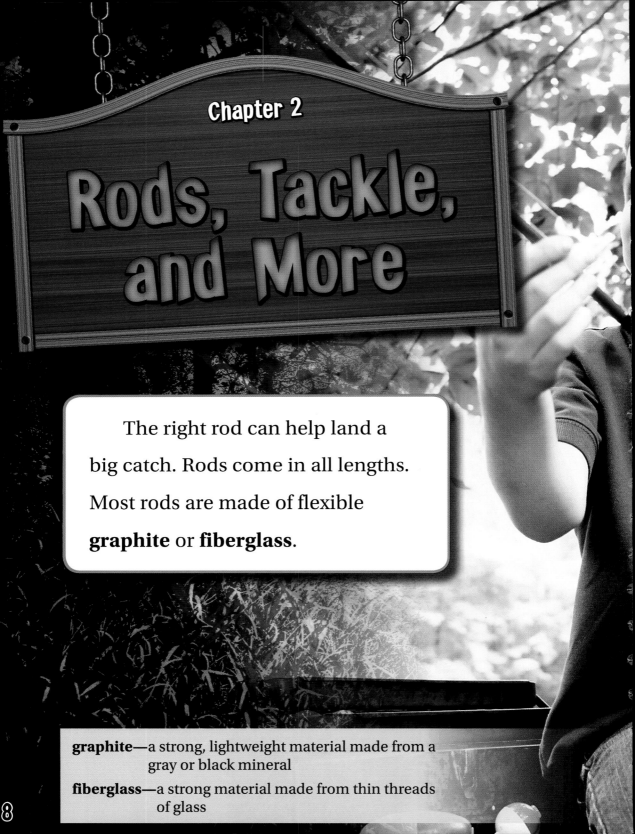

Chapter 2

Rods, Tackle, and More

The right rod can help land a big catch. Rods come in all lengths. Most rods are made of flexible **graphite** or **fiberglass**.

graphite—a strong, lightweight material made from a gray or black mineral

fiberglass—a strong material made from thin threads of glass

rod

Wild Fact:

Some fishing rods are as short as your arm. Others are twice as tall as a basketball hoop.

reel

The clear fishing line fools fish into thinking they are chasing real food.

guide

Fishing line is spooled around a reel. The clear line is threaded through guides along the rod. The bigger the fish, the thicker and stronger the line must be.

Anglers tie hooks at the end of the line. Hooks hold bait and have sharp **barbs**. Earthworms and grubs make good bait. Minnows look like a tasty meal for larger fish.

hook

minnows

worms

grubs

barb—the sharp point that sticks backward from the tip of the hook and helps snag the fish

Some anglers use **lures** to hook prize fish. Lures move like prey to catch a fish's attention. **Bobbers** dip underwater to show when fish bite. Bobbers also keep bait from dragging on the bottom of the water.

lure—man-made bait used for fishing
bobber—a floating ball attached to the fishing line

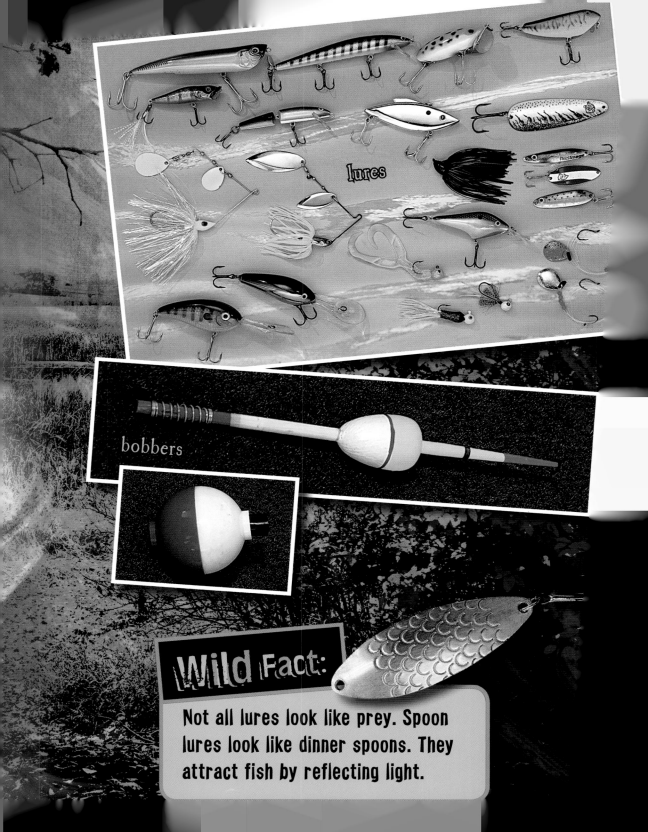

lures

bobbers

Wild Fact:

Not all lures look like prey. Spoon lures look like dinner spoons. They attract fish by reflecting light.

fiberglass rod

jacket

sunglasses

life vest

bait

tackle box

net

lures

fishing license

bobber

16

Freshwater Fishing Equipment

depth finder

vest

bait bucket

baitcasting reel

sunscreen

spincasting reel

fishing line

17

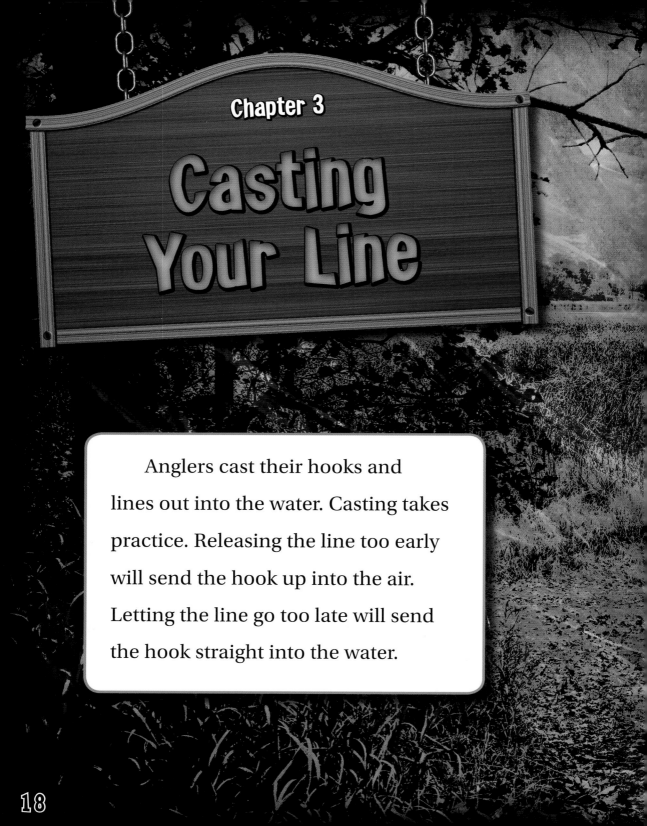

Chapter 3

Casting Your Line

Anglers cast their hooks and lines out into the water. Casting takes practice. Releasing the line too early will send the hook up into the air. Letting the line go too late will send the hook straight into the water.

Slowly reeling in the line makes the bait or lure seem alive. The wiggling bait attracts fish. Once the fish bites, anglers set the hook. They quickly pull up and back on the rod.

Wild Fact:

Most states limit the size, number, or type of fish people can catch and keep.

Wild Fact:

The world record for the largest striped bass ever caught was 78.5 pounds (36 kilograms). The angler took nearly two hours to land the catch.

Reeling in a **lunker** takes extra work. Anglers use nets to help haul in monster catches. A net helps lift the huge fish from the water. Nets ease the strain on rods and lines.

lunker—a fish that is unusually large for its kind

Chapter 4

Safety First

Safety comes first for anglers. Hooks are as sharp as needles. Anglers watch out for others and look before casting. They are careful when removing the fish from the hook.

Wild Fact:

Pike are fish that have razor-sharp teeth. Anglers use pliers or special tools to remove hooks from these fish.

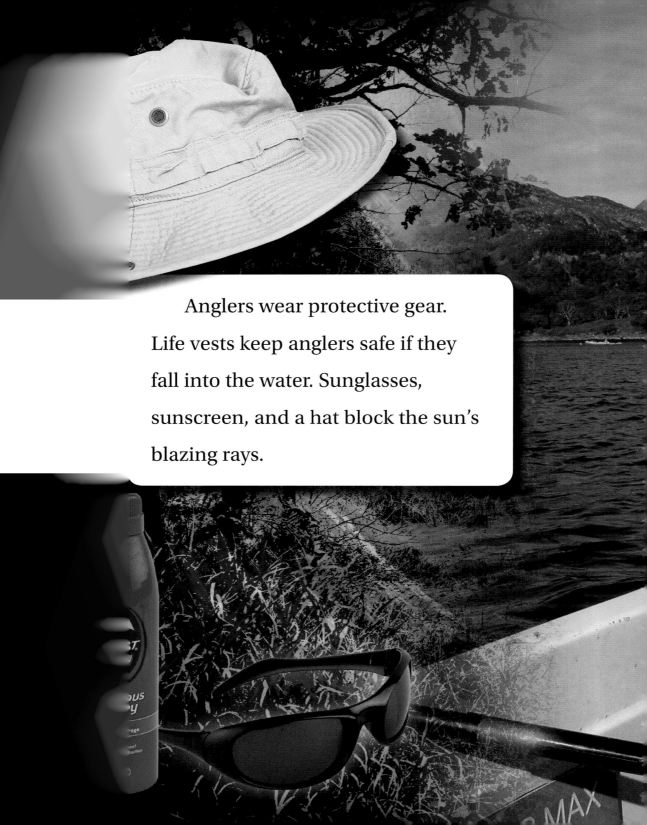

Anglers wear protective gear. Life vests keep anglers safe if they fall into the water. Sunglasses, sunscreen, and a hat block the sun's blazing rays.

Chapter 5

Reel in Some Fun!

Catch-and-release fishing is earth-friendly and fun. Or maybe you want to **clean** your catch and fry it for a feast. Pack up your tackle and go fishing!

catch-and-release—setting a fish free after catching it
clean—to remove a fish's scales, fins, and insides before cooking it

Glossary

angler (ANG-gler)—a person who fishes with a hook and line

bait (BAYT)—a small amount of food used to attract a fish or animal so you can catch it

barb (BAHRB)—the sharp point that sticks backward from the tip of the hook and helps snag the fish

bobber (BOB-ur)—a floating ball fixed to the fishing line

catch-and-release (KACH-AND-ri-LEESS)—to catch a fish and set it free instead of keeping it

clean (KLEEN)—to remove a fish's scales, fins, and insides before preparing it to eat

fiberglass (FY-buhr-glas)—a strong material made from thin threads of glass

freshwater (FRESH-wah-tuhr)—water that has little or no salt; most ponds, rivers, lakes, and streams have freshwater

graphite (GRA-fite)—a strong, lightweight material made from a gray or black mineral

lunker (LUHNG-ker)—a fish that is unusually large for its kind

lure (LOOR)—man-made bait used for fishing

prey (PRAY)—an animal hunted by another animal for food

tackle (TAK-uhl)—the equipment needed for fishing

Read More

Hopkins, Ellen. *Freshwater Fishing*. The Great Outdoors. Mankato, Minn.: Capstone Press, 2008.

Kelley, K. C. *Let's Go Fishing*. Boys' Life Series. New York: DK, 2008.

Ross, Nick. *Fishing*. Get Outdoors. New York: PowerKids Press, 2010.

Internet Sites

FactHound offers a safe, fun way to find Internet sites related to this book. All of the sites on FactHound have been researched by our staff.

Here's all you do:

Visit *www.facthound.com*

Type in this code: **9781429648103**

Index